ISLAMIC RUGS

KUDRET H. TURKHAN

Edited by Lynne Thornton

ARTHUR BARKER LIMITED
5 Winsley Street London W1

Copyright © 1968 by Kudret H. Turkhan
SBN 213 76473 3
Designed by Behram Kapadia
Illustrations printed gravure by D. H. Greaves Ltd.
Text printed and bound by C. Tinling & Co. Ltd,
Liverpool, London and Prescot

I dedicate this book to my wife and to her father, the late Mr Elia Perez, who played such an important part in the international carpet trade. He created a firm without equal after a long and difficult struggle and was considered one of the best known authorities on this subject.

contents

illustrations

B

ACKNOWLEDGEMENTS

The illustrations appearing on the pages listed above are reproduced by kind permission of the following: The British Museum: page 43; Islamic Museum, Istanbul: page 66; The National Gallery: pages 14, 15; The Top-Kapi Museum: pages 68, 69, 72; Miss Olga Ford: page 21; Messrs Perez (London) Ltd.: pages 13, 16, 24, 33, 35, 36, 42, 46, 47, 54, 56 (top), 58, 59 (top), 60 (top), 65, 71, 77, 78 (bottom), 80, 89, 90, 91, 92, 99, 102, 105; Messrs Sotheby & Co.: 22, 23, 34, 41, 44, 45, 48, 53, 55, 56 (bottom), 57, 59 (bottom), 60 (bottom), 67, 70, 78 (top), 79, 100, 101, 103, 104, 106.

introduction

What is the significance of a rug? Where, when and by whom were they made? For we Oriental people, rugs explain many things. Through them can be read the whole history of tribes, their days of war and domination, their cultures, religion and finally their decadence. When an Oriental wishes to learn about rugs, he does not seek the help of books but rather turns to the rugs themselves and to the dealers in the bazaars, for he knows that a comprehensive and accurate knowledge cannot be obtained from books alone. It is the rugs themselves that must be studied, their appearance, the types of wool used, the method and style of knotting and – something a book can never teach – the very *feel* of each individual type when handled.

The acquiring of such knowledge is a long and complicated business and for the true expert it means many years of wearying and uncomfortable travel, often by most primitive methods, through the heart of Asia, calling at the numerous villages and towns where the art is carried on. Sometimes it calls for long journeys to visit the nomadic tribes who weave their sturdy and often sombrely beautiful rugs for use in their everyday life. The people of the Orient are lucky in having examples all around them, as dealers and their wares are an everyday sight, but for the people of other lands it is no simple matter and it is in order to help these that books are written.

I myself have spent my whole life handling rugs. I am a Turk from the Caucasus and it was near Hile, a small village 250 miles from Baku on the peninsular of Apsheron, that my grandfather, an important chieftain, had a large estate where he kept one of the finest collections of rugs one could imagine. My childhood was spent surrounded by these wonderful pieces and I would listen to my grandfather, Aga Shamsi Bey Assadullah Zade, and the rest of the family, nearly all of whom were great experts, discussing rugs, their provenance and the craftmanship that had gone into their making. But however much one learns from books and museums, to be an expert one must be able to appreciate beauty. I remember as a child in 1916 visiting an uncle on *Bairam*, the day of the Festival of Sacrifice, when it is customary for the young to see respected relations in order to kiss their hands. Hadji Zein-ulm Abdin was a powerful leading figure among Azerbaidjanian Turks and he enjoyed collecting fine Oriental art. Four years earlier he had bought at an auction in St Petersburg a carpet for which he paid something like 75,000 roubles, having outbid even the famous Russian collector, Count Stroganoff. The carpet was one of the finest examples of early seventeenth-century weaving from the Persian Imperial Court workshops, made for the Polish market. When I came in front of Uncle Hadji I could not answer any of his questions about my lessons or future plans for study, as my whole mind was occupied with the magnificent carpet, which lay in front of his gilded throne. It was knotted in silk in light turquoise and green, blue and delicate rose, gleaming with gold threads. Mama, embarrassed, said 'Kudret, what's the matter? Don't you see enough carpets?' I, without knowing where it came from, its value or age, replied in a voice trembling with emotion, 'But Mama, that is a real gem. Even in Grand-papa's house there is not such a splendour.' My uncle looked with great satisfaction first at me and then at my mother and said '*Hanim* (lady). I can see your son has a feeling for beautiful things,' and to me, 'Kudret, I promise you that this carpet is no more mine, but yours. When you own your own house, you will have it and until then I will enjoy it.' I wonder if it still lies in his palace, now the State Museum of Baku?

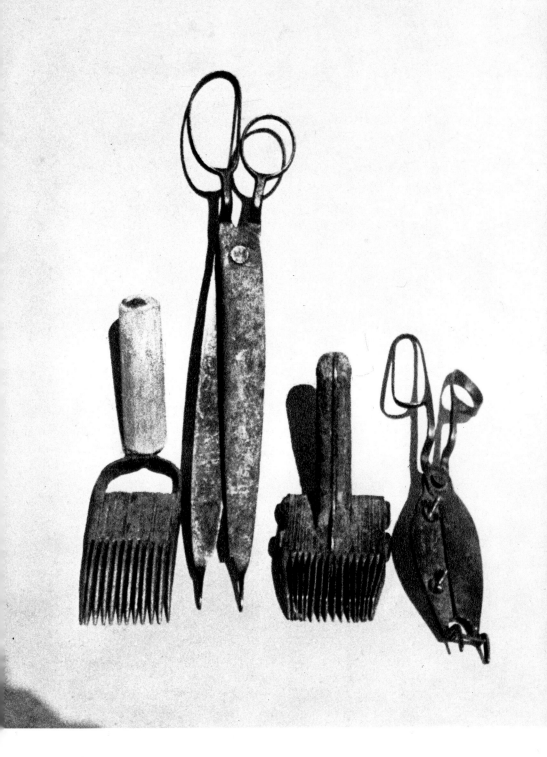

Instruments used by the weaver

Willem Duyster, 'Man and woman playing tric-trac', early 17th century, (Detail) showing an Oushak carpet

Yarn being spun by hand

Young weavers at a loom

1

GENERAL BACKGROUND

How to acquire a knowledge of rugs

The first step should be simply to learn how to distinguish the main groups of rugs. There are six of these: Turkish, Caucasian, Persian, Central Asian, Indian and Chinese. Then there are the individual types within these groups. As there are not only well over one hundred different kinds, but weavers of more modern times have also imitated other styles, this becomes more complicated. The third stage of study is most important, as one must be able to differentiate between the several grades of rugs which may be made in one centre and to pick out the really antique rugs from those which are perhaps a hundred years old, those which have some age, and those modern productions which have had a good deal of wear. Lastly, it is necessary to be able to detect both new rugs which have been chemically treated in order to give them the appearance of age, and those which are actually woven forgeries, fakes of rare and valuable pieces.

I would advise you first of all to go to a reliable dealer and ask him to explain the fundamental points. Then visit the museum to set yourself a high standard and to the auctioneers' galleries to see a variety of good and bad, and read such books as Dr Martin's *Oriental Rugs*, John K. Mumford's *Oriental Rugs*, Dr Bode's *Antique Rugs from the Near East* and Dr Orendi's *Orientalische Teppiche*. Then go back to look at the rugs themselves to fix the knowledge acquired firmly in your memory.

A brief history

Precisely when knotted rugs were first made has never been satisfactorily established. Although ancient records mention carpets at the time of Cyrus in the sixth century BC, these may have been felt or pileless coverings. Recently some interesting discoveries have been made at Pazyryk in the Altai mountains of Siberia where fragments of a rug were found, perhaps 2,400 years old, exceptionally preserved in hard-packed ice. There is no doubt that by the sixth century AD real masterpieces were being woven, the best known being the vast carpet of the Sassanian Emperor Chosroes who had it worked with a representation of a garden with trees, flowers and running water in gold and silver thread, silk and precious stones, so that during the Winter months he could believe that it was Spring inside his palace. The only other existing early examples of pile carpets we have date from a period long after the Islamic Empire had been established and the Mohammedan religion had spread throughout the Middle East.

Although it must have been nomadic tribes who first wove coverings with thick pile to protect them against the bitter cold of the mountains, very soon

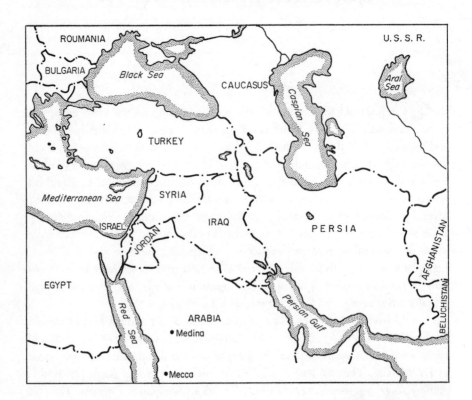

there were not only rugs made in and for the home, but those commissioned by merchants and those made on a grand scale in workshops attached to palaces. In Oriental painted miniatures of the fifteenth century holy men, heroes and sages sit or kneel on rugs of rich and imaginative design, while in the West, many six-teenth-century artists depicted identifiable rugs from Asia Minor, with which a lively trade was carried on. Venetian inventories list as many as ten carpets in the larger houses and all the great Princes of Europe had their collection. The carpets were considered too valuable to be put on the floor but were draped over tables and benches, hung from balconies on gala occasions and used to decorate gondolas.

Of the three main groups I will discuss, the Persian weavers proved to be masters of curves, symmetry, rhythm and intricate design; the Turks showed their artistry by using rare shades and simple patterns full of charm, and the half savage folk of Caucasia combined richness of colour and geometric drawing with their great technical knowledge of how to produce the best wool.

Dyeing

Colours are of great significance to all Eastern people and one of the most important is turquoise – a stone that from the poorest to the richest is used to protect them
from bad luck or misfortune. Even today in Turkey or Persia you can see tur-
quoises worn by nomads, children and animals, and even in taxis a piece hangs in
front of the driver. My car has one for safety and because of this tradition my
wife's engagement ring was turquoise. Another very important but rarely used
colour in a Mohammedan rug is green, this being sacred to the Prophet
Mohammed. White, especially unusual in prayer rugs, stands for peace and tran-
quillity, while red is the national colour of the Turks and is symbolic of glory,
strength and bravery. Yellow indicates wealth and worldly success; black, the
national colour of the Mongols and Tartars, also signifies fighting and war; rose,
for the Turkomans, represents dignity, and blue, Destiny.

Each nomadic dyer has his own professional secrets and this knowledge, viewed
as a sacred treasure, is passed from its possessor to the heir of the family. No dyer
keeps his recipes recorded in a notebook, but carries them in his head. Plants,
flowers, fruit, vegetables and even some insects were the principal sources of the
hasboya or vegetable dyes used in all old rugs. As far as we know, red comes from
madder roots, kermes (a beetle found in cacti) and cochineal; blue from the indigo
plant or from *isatis tinctoria*. This plant, the woad of the Ancient Britons, is quite
common in Anatolia and is cut before flowering, being then kept in water for
about three to four hours in order to give a strong, brilliant colour. Yellow comes
from sumach, saffron stamens, onion skins, burberry and vine leaves; green from
nuts, willow leaves and extracts of different fruits; orange from henna, narsingar
flowers or the jack-wood tree, used in Burma for dyeing the orange cloth worn
by Buddhist monks; purple from cherry branches; white is natural wool; black,
natural goat hair and walnut dye; brown, natural camel hair, walnut leaves,
gallnut and nut shells.

When a rug has been made, the dyes are set fast by being left in cold water
until the excess colour has run out, and in villages where there is a stream, one
can see the rugs suspended by ropes between each bank or kneaded under the feet
of the men and afterwards left to dry in the sun.

Aniline dyes

It was in Persia that aniline dyes first came into use sometime around 1880-90,
but a strict law was made by Nasreddin Shah, himself a great patron of fine arts,
that no synthetic dyes should be used in the manufacture of carpets. Failure to
observe the law met with severe punishment. Unfortunately by the end of the
First World War, a great many people were again using the cheaper but unsatis-
factory and harsh aniline dyes. These tend to run and lack the mellow, deep

richness of the old vegetable dyes which today are still produced and used in
several places in Turkey such as Yahji-Bediz, Jahyali and Yuruk.

Abrash

When there is a variation of the same colour in a rug, it is called an *abrash*; this
can be seen mainly in old pieces, especially in tribal fabrics. Many collectors and
lovers of primitive art prefer a rug with an *abrash* and certainly do not consider it
a defect. It generally results from tribal migration, when the dyeing process is
affected by the quality of the plants and water and the wool becoming either
harder or softer with the different grazing.

The Boyadji, or Dyer

Everything has now changed, but the inherited profession of a *boyadji* or dyer
(who was nearly always a man) was a noble and respected one. In the family, the
halef (inheritor) began his training first as a *yamak* (assistant's assistant), becoming
a *yardimji* (assistant) and then a *tchirak* (learner). After a long practical training he
was called a *boyadji*. If, after some years, during which time he had created some
good, original colours of his own, then only did he take the name of *usta*, or
master.

Preparation

The foundation threads (warp and weft) on which the pile is built up, are wool
in Turkey and Caucasia and cotton, wool and silk in Persia. These materials, with
the addition of goat and camel hair, are used for the actual body of the rug. After
the wool has been prepared and dyed, it is spun. A primitive spindle is used, about
ten to fourteen inches long. Near its point is attached a ball of unbaked clay to
give it weight in turning. The spinner twists it between thumb and forefinger of
one hand while he or she draws out the single filaments from the bundles of wool
and twists them into yarn upon the spindle.

Weaving

Rugs are woven on looms, which are basically frames on to which warp threads
are tightly stretched from upper to lower struts. Although the looms in factories
are vertical, with a roller at one end, in the villages and amongst nomadic tribes
they are horizontal, and in primitive conditions may be little more than four
branches bound together with twine.

From the balls of wool, the weaver binds a piece of thread round two warp
threads from the back, pulling it tight so the loose ends are in the front and then
with a special knife, cuts off the yarn after the knot is made. A horizontal (weft)

(opposite) Mihrab in the mosque of Sokollu Cami, Istanbul

(*left*) Inscription cartouches

Detail of the *mihrab* of an antique prayer rug

(*opposite*) Detail of the *mihrab* of a later rug

A silk Tabriz prayer rug

thread is passed through, usually after two rows of knots, and with a heavy iron comb is beaten against the previously completed work. The weaver will then clip smooth the ends of the yarn after each row is finished with a special pair of shears.

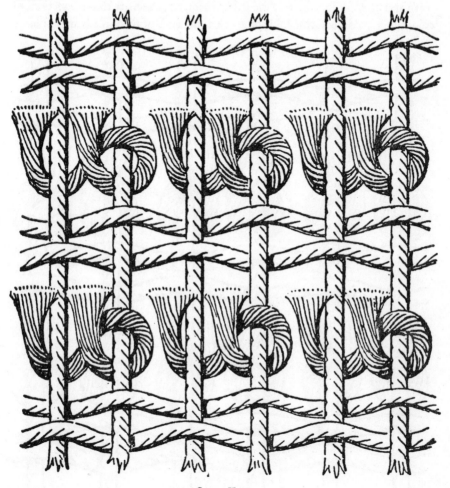

Senne Knot

There are two kinds of knots, the Ghiordes and the Senne. The Ghiordes (Turkish) full knot has the yarn twisted about the warp threads in such a way that the two raised ends of the pile alternate with every two threads of the warp. This is generally used by weavers in Turkey, Caucasia and Transcaspia, while the Persians use the Senne as well. The Senne (Persian) half knot, which has the advantage that it can be tied to either the right or to the left, has a piece of pile dividing each warp thread.

While Caucasian and Turkish rugs generally have a flat selvage about a quarter of an inch wide at each side of the rug, the Persians ones are overbound in dark red or blue wool, and the nomadic tribes in brown.

Kelims

The *kelim* is a pileless rug. The different coloured weft threads are taken across the warp and back for just the area the pattern requires, so where the two sections of colour meet, a slit is formed. In some *kelims* the ends of the threads are left loose

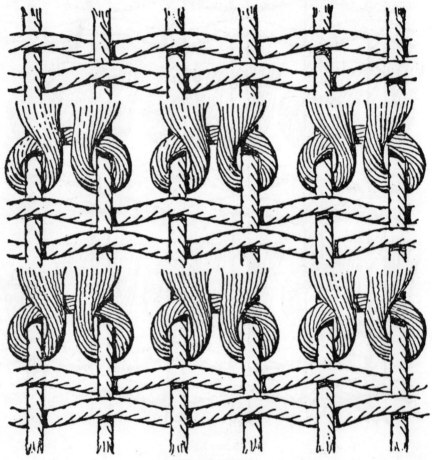

Ghiordes Knot

on the back, like a European tapestry, but generally they are incorporated into the weaving so that the rug can be used on either side. Many *kelims* are woven in two or three strips or *kanats* which are then sewn together, but as this is not always done very carefully, the designs are irregular. Children are often employed as weavers as they can tie finer knots. In Persia, girls of six or seven begin by learning how to roll and pass the yarn. They then learn to beat down the rows of knots after the weft has been thrown through and by the age of nine they are permitted to work at the loom itself. No matter how poor the family is, a rug is found in nearly every home, its beauty in striking contrast to the surrounding misery.

Designing

An unsolved mystery concerning Oriental rugs is how the *kalfas* or designers, without any education in drawing or painting, are able to produce the most wonderful harmonic patterns. In such great centres of the industry as Tabriz in

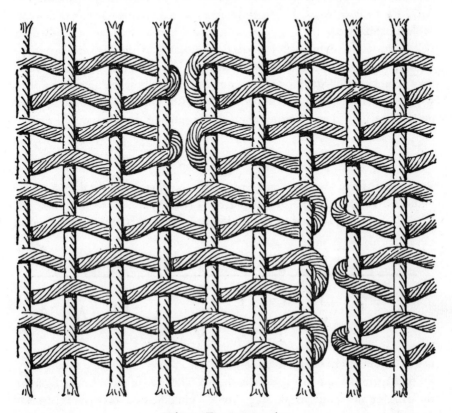

Kelim or Tapestry weaving

Persia or Smyrna (Izmir) in Turkey, coloured designs are distributed among the weavers at the loom, but in the tribal areas it is the *kalfa* himself who 'conducts' the weaving, just as the conductor of an orchestra controls the colour and texture of the music.

It was in Transcaspia that I first saw how the *kalfa* directs the making of a rug. First, he begins with a prayer to send away the Evil Eye and then in a gentle melancholic tone he dictates patterns and colours. Four young girls at the loom were working so rapidly that I could hardly follow them with my eyes. The *kalfa's* gentle words were, 'Weave, my young gazelles, do your best. Your beauty will be admired through it by thousands of brave and true believers.' Later, when I became friendly with him, I asked him how many designs he knew. He said that it was about forty and in order to prove it, drew several of them on the sand in a few minutes. He also told me that boys are lazy and no good at weaving; the best workers are young girls.

I have often been asked about the irregularities found in rugs, as some people believe they are defective for this reason. One must remember that antique and semi-antique rugs were mostly knotted by primitive people living in high mountains and vast steppes, far away from the influences of Western civilisations, who wove for their own use and to their native taste. Another factor is that the Mohammedan weavers are superstitious, believing that anything perfectly done will be cursed, as only Allah is perfect. Also, many of the rugs are woven by young girls or women who know the pattern by heart and, as it is repetitive work, they do not pay full attention to the knotting, especially when they are mothers with young children. Finally, rugs of the nomads are taken out of the loom, rolled up for days on end and then remounted, thus pulling the work out of shape.

Numbers

Rugs, particularly Caucasian ones, are sometimes woven with the date in Arabic numerals. The Mohammedan date, which of course does not correspond to the Christian calendar, is based on the year of the *hegira* in AD 622 when the Prophet

0	1	2	3	4	5	6	7	8	9
•	١	٢	٣	٤	٥	٦	٧	٨	٩

fled to Medina from the persecution of the pagan rulers of Mecca. Accordingly, AD 1968 corresponds to AH 1388 (*anno hegira*). The style of these Arabic figures is the same for all Islamic people except for a slight difference between Persian and Turkish.

The Armenian weavers in Turkey use Arabic for the date, but in the Karabag district of Caucasia they use Christian numbers and Armenian letters when the rugs are signed.

Inscriptions

The maker's signature is seldom found except for a few examples such as the famous Ardebil carpet by Maksoud in the Victoria and Albert Museum, but in Persia, carpets were worked with phrases from the Koran and the *Shah-Nameh* (Book of Kings) or verses from the *Rubayat* of Omar Khayyam and Sa'dis' *Gulistan*. In Turkey they would inscribe the name of God, the Prophet or principal phrases from the Koran, the holy book of Islam. What is found in Turkish art one does not find in Persian, for it was created by a people who had always to be prepared for war and so had little time left for joy and smiles. Even today we are a reserved nation and our art is mostly dedicated to religious purposes where strict observance is demanded.

Sizes

Apart from their division into main groups and sub-groups according to their origin, Oriental rugs are still further differentiated by size, each having its particular name and function in Middle Eastern houses. Among these are saddle bags (*hurj*), couch covers (*yastik*), rugs for corridors (*yan*) and runners for passage ways (*kenare*), but the names I have used most are *namazlik*, rugs used for praying on, *kelleyi*, small rugs and *saphs*, long rugs or carpets used for covering mosque floors. Perhaps I should explain here that although the words rug and carpet have been used in a general way to describe woven fabric with pile, a rug is generally taken as being 6 feet by 4 feet. Anything over that size becomes either a carpet or a runner.

Prayer rugs

Mohammed, who founded the religion of Islam (the word means 'I submit to the will of God') was not only a Prophet, but a leader, judge and military general. His successors were called the Caliphs and his followers, Moslems, or adherents of Islam. The Koran, the holy book, embodies all his teachings, and the *Hadith* (traditions), his sayings and decisions. The ban on the representation of human and animal forms did not exist in early Islam but appears to have developed towards the end of the eighth century. At that time there was a tradition that, 'On the Day of Judgement the punishment of hell will be meted out to the painter and he will be called upon to breathe life into the forms he has fashioned.' Disagreement about the succession of the Caliphs divided Moslems into orthodox Sunnis and Sh'ias. Sunnis respected the pictorial veto and it resulted in a religious art with highly ornamental abstract and caligraphic decoration, but in the secular art of the Sh'ias, among whom are the Persians, human and animal forms combine with flowers and plants.

Mosques all face Mecca, the centre of Islam which is symbolised by the Kaaba, a pre-Moslem sanctuary towards which Mohammedans turn to pray. In each mosque there is a *kibla* wall with a central niche or *mihrab*, which faces Mecca.

Prayer rugs – a rug for the worshipper to kneel on during prayer – were made with a design of a mosque *mihrab*. Sometimes the corners (spandrels) of the niche were woven with representations of combs and ewers, reminding the faithful of their duty of cleanliness, or, particularly in Caucasian rugs, a stylised hand, either to indicate the position of the hands during prayer or as a symbolic hand of Fatima, the daughter of Mohammed. The sides of the *mihrab* in the rug often had columns resembling large candlesticks and a lamp hanging from the apex of the niche, both to be found in the mosque itself. In antique prayer rugs these motifs are quite realistic but by the late eighteenth century they degenerate into columns of carnations and bunches of flowers.

Prayer rugs are mostly found in Asia Minor, where the *mihrab* niche is tall and curving in the earlier examples, becoming flatter and more angular later on. Caucasian prayer rugs are quite common. The niche is always completely geometric and the *mihrab* has no columns at the sides. The remarkable Turkish rugs made in Kum-Kapu and Hereke during the latter part of the nineteenth century were thought for a long time to be antique Persian prayer rugs which are very rare, as the Persians used cotton or linen mats to pray on. One sees many rugs from Persia woven with a *mihrab*-shaped field, but these are too large to have ever been carried about and were woven purely for decorative purposes.

This story will show how much a prayer rug means to an Oriental. In 1917 I went with my grandfather on a tour of inspection of his cotton plantations and factories between Kizil-Arvat and Tashkent in Transcaspia. We were staying with one of the head chiefs of the nomadic tribes, Mir Ahmed Emir Han, and the huge tent which formed our bedroom was hung with nothing but superb Turkoman rugs. One of these was offered to my grandfather for use as a prayer rug and, startled by its beauty, he said, 'Son, you have already seen many splendours at home, but what you now admire you will never see again.' It was a unique silk rug woven in the manner of the Pindé tribe, the top border with the inscription, *Lâ ilâh illâ Allâh – Mohammed rasûl Allah* ('There is no god but God – Mohammed is His Prophet'). The Emir told us that it had been made by his grandmother while she was awaiting the birth of his father and, as he had no heir, he would consider it an honour if we would take it in memory of our stay with him. The Grand Duke Nicolai Nicolaievich, then Viceroy of Caucasia, was one our guests and when he saw the rug he begged my grandfather to let him buy it, but he said 'You can have anything in the house except that rug, Your Imperial Highness. You are not of our religion and it would bring bad luck to you as well as to my grandchild.'

Saphs

These are long rugs or carpets woven with *mihrabs* placed side by side. It is sometimes thought that they were used as family prayer rugs but the *mihrabs* are too narrow and they were in fact woven to cover mosque floors. Such carpets can be of great size and in 1674 one with 132 *mihrabs* was recorded as being in the Yeni Walide mosque in Istanbul. They are not often found, and the only places where they seem to have been woven are Oushak, Mudjur and the Anatolian mountains in Turkey, or in Khotan and Samarkand in Turkestan.

The value of rugs

Until one has seen many rugs and can recognise the good from the bad, it is difficult to know why one piece is more valuable than another, particularly when they are overpraised by people anxious to sell their nondescript, fourth-rate wares. Although the fineness of the weave must be taken into consideration, this quality is not often found in antiques, and they cannot be condemned on that account. In modern rugs, especially those in silk, fineness *is* important, for the pattern will not only be more clearly defined but the rug itself will last longer. The design should be beautiful and the colours good, for even though bright colours are placed side by side, they should harmonize, unlike the shrill oranges and pinks found in some modern examples.

Buying

When buying a rug, it is wise to deal only with a reputable firm, preferably with one that has been personally recommended to you. Or, go with someone who has a knowlege of rugs and who can give you good advice. One should beware of 'great bargains' from unknown dealers or firms, for many people have been persuaded to buy poorly woven rugs for enormous prices by clever salesmen.

There are a number of common defects it is as well to look out for. If you turn over a corner of the rug diagonally, face inwards, and gently twist it, you will hear a cracking sound if the rug is 'faulty'. This is because it has perished after having become damp and not being dried out properly. One also comes across this sound in silk rugs, Sennas, Zilli-Sultans, Sarouks and other delicate rugs whose foundation threads are too fine for the weight of the pile. They can be backed with some stout material and hung on the wall, but are obviously impractical for use on the floor. There are rugs made with synthetic (aniline) dyes which are washed in acid in order to bleach them and to simulate faded vegetable dyes, but a quick look at the back will show you that some of the harsh colouring still remains. An antique rug obviously cannot have aniline dyes, as they only came in during the late nineteenth century. Other rugs have been cut where they are too badly worn, and the edges cleverly sewn together. Again, the back will show where this has been done and it is advisable to check when you find a rug of unusual size for its type. Another way of concealing wear is by painting the rug, but this can be detected by noticing if the darker colours have run into the white or by rubbing the suspicious place with a cloth wetted with saliva. The colour will also stain the cloth if the dyes are poor and the rug has not been washed properly after weaving to 'set' them. Something that is not so often encountered is a fake, *i.e.* a rug which has been made to look antique in order to deceive. Holes are made in the fabric by burning or rubbing with pumice stone but these are not usually consistent with natural wear. The fringe of a rug is often replaced but if it is original and looks new, this may indicate that the whole rug is of recent manufacture. Another sign of a genuine antique is that the knotting will have a corrugated appearance on the back. Sometimes these fakes are difficult to spot. Both the seventeenth-century 'bird' Oushaks and 'Transylvanian' rugs (*q.v.*) were copied with great skill near Bucharest in the 1920s by a man named Tudok. They were included in bales of older pieces and were sold in London in good faith as genuine antiques.

Carpets are now made by machine and, unless you want to buy them for practical use in the house, they should be avoided. Long warp threads are woven into the fabric and left standing up in loops, which are then cut through in order to simulate hand-knotted pile carpets. The pattern des not show clearly on the back, which will have a greyish look. The fringe at each end is always applied and when one of the 'knots' is pulled hard, it will come out.

After you have satisfied yourself that the rug you wish to buy has none of these defects, you should make sure that it lies flat on the floor and is not irregularly shaped, that there are no patches or stains and if there is any wear, that it is equal all over the rug.

Maintenance and repair

Minor repairs can be carried out quickly and cheaply, but major repairs are expensive and they lower the value of the rug. Particular attention should be paid to the edges of a rug because if these are allowed to become ragged, the pile itself will start to fall apart. One of the main causes of wear in old rugs is that sharp gritty substances work their way down through the pile and into the knots, eventually, through constantly being trodden in, cutting through them and leaving the warp and weft exposed. This can be averted to a great extent by cleaning the rug from the back with a vacuum cleaner which will remove all the dust and grit without harming the pile. This can also be done by placing the rug face down on newspaper or a lawn and gently beating the back with a carpet beater.

The natural fats and oils in the wool will dry up if the rug is neglected. The wool will then become harsh and brittle, begin to disintegrate, and the pile will wear away. Hand cleaning with a good household soap (not detergent), is the answer to this. Just enough water to make a lather should be used and in no circumstances should the rug be soaked. Carpet cleaning machines with rotary action should be avoided as they use too much water and the dirt is left to seep into the back of the carpet, eventually rotting the foundation threads. Since large carpets are more of a problem to clean, the best plan is to get in touch with a good carpet dealer who will either take it away and clean it for you or arrange to have it done at home. It is anyway a good idea to have all your rugs cleaned professionally once a year.

If something is spilt on the rug, it should be absorbed with blotting paper or material and then gently dabbed with a cloth dampened with white spirit or soap and water. Detergent should never be used, as this will only cause a larger stain. If you can, get in touch with a dealer who will be able to advise you how to deal with the spillage.

Your Oriental rug will not only be a pleasure to have in your home but will increase in value, for every year, as the standard of living improves in the Middle East, men and women prefer an easy, clean job in a modern factory to sitting in front of a primitive loom and weaving their traditional art.

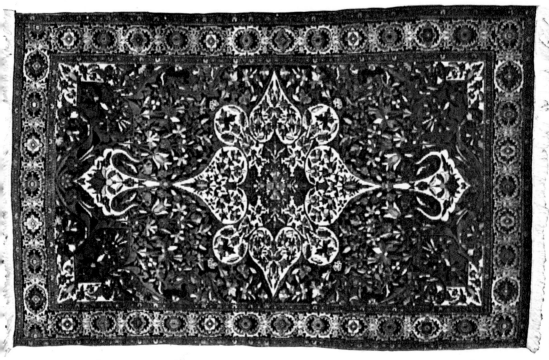

A Sarouk rug, the field woven with a pole-medallion

A Zilli-Sultan rug

Detail of a *mihrab* of a 17th
century Turkish prayer rug

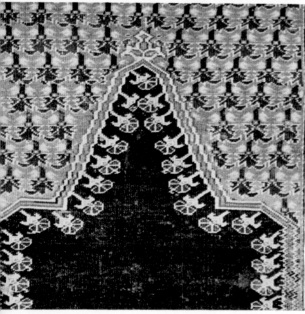

An 18th century Turkish
prayer rug

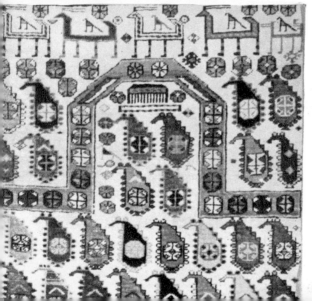

A 19th century Caucasian
prayer rug

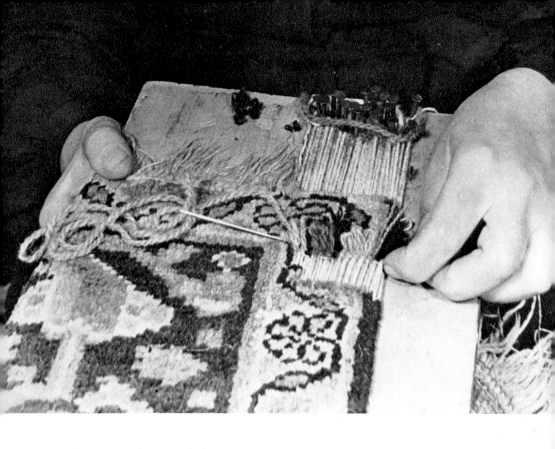

(*above*) A rug during and (*below*) after repair

2

PERSIA

Persia, or as it is called today, Iran, is bordered by Mesopotamia, Asia Minor and the Caucasus in the west, Soviet Central Asia in the north and Afghanistan and Baluchistan on the east. Crossed by one of the oldest trade routes, the Silk Road, Persia was the centre of communications between the East and the West but was for this very reason open to invasion. Great dynasties seized power and ruled this vast country, from the Achaeminids in the seventh century BC under such kings as Cyrus and Darius, to the Sassanians, who were defeated by the Arab armies in AD 640. Already most of Asia Minor and Egypt had been overwhelmed and the Sassanians were easily converted from their ancient religion of Zoroastrianism to that of the newly-founded Islam.

Although now unified through her religion with the surrounding countries, Persia was still torn by war. In the eleventh century the Turkish Seljuks took over control from the Buyids, only to be themselves slaughtered and their capital Rayy destroyed by the invading Mongols from the East under Ghengis Khan. The conquerors, who killed tens of thousands of Moslems and razed whole cities,

(*opposite*) An antique Oushak rug of the 'Holbein' type

were converted to Islam and set up Tabriz as their capital. Under the direction of their leader, they built many houses with mosques, universities and libraries. There was a second Mongolian invasion in the fourteenth century under Timur (Tamerlane) from near Samarkand and it was not until 1502 that a Persian dynasty ruled Iran again with the Safavid Shah Ismail.

Historians tell us that pile carpets were being woven in Persia in the seventh century, but it is from the time of the Safavids that the masterpieces of weaving survive, the result of traditions inherited from the ancient world enhanced by new inspiration from the East. This great period in Persian art was dominated by the Shahs Ismail (1502-24), Tahmasp (1524-76), who moved the capital from Tabriz to Kasvin to evade the Ottoman Turks, and Abbas I (1587-1629), who moved to Ispahan. The first carpets of this time were worked with intricate arabesques forming abstract spirals intertwined with small leaves and animals. The designing of carpets was the work not of craftsmen but of artists such as Riza-i-Abbah and the renowned Behzad of Herat, who became director of the bibliophile academy in Tabriz. These Court painters were able to adapt their lively and realistic drawing from the miniature scale of book bindings and manu-

Henna flower   Stylised cones

scripts to the monamental, and the carpets became huge paintings in wool. In one group the whole field is covered with palmettes and flowers growing in vases. Others are worked with a repetitive design called 'Shah Abbas', in honour of the ruler, with flowerheads and cloud bands (derived from the traditional Chinese motif for representing clouds). The 'compartment' carpets have birds, cloud bands and sprays of blossom enclosed by quatrefoils. There is the *herati* design which takes its name from the city of Herat, with rows of flowerheads edged with large palm-like leaves, and the 'Gulli Henna' design with sprigs of henna flowers. Not only were carpets worked with brightly coloured flowers and leaves, but glazed tiles of the buildings, clothes, sword scabbards, armour, cushions, hangings and tents; all repeat the same highly manneristic decoration. Inspiration for other carpet designs was drawn from Persian legends and literature, such as the story of the lovers Laila and Madjnun, the Rauzat-ous-Safu by Sa'di, the Shah-Nameh and the Zafer-Nameh. Another variety of carpets from this period are woven with a stylised garden, perhaps traditional adaptations of the fabled 'winter carpet' of the Sassanian Emperor Chosroes. Hunting was a favourite sport of the Court, and carpets for the last four hundred years have copied the Safavid sporting scenes in which princes and attendants with falcons on their wrists ride through forests of flowers and scrolls while leopards, tigers and dragons attack spotted ibex and boar. In contrast to this savagery, the wide borders sometimes contain genii or angels with outspread wings who sit cross-legged, gossiping and serving each other with drinks.

One of the most famous Safavid carpets is now in the Victoria and Albert Museum in London. It was made at Shah Tahmasp's direction for the sepulchral mosque in Ardebil where his father was buried, and besides the date AH 946 (AD 1540), it has this inscription and signature: *I have no refuge in the world other than Thy threshold. My head has no protection other than this porchway. The work of the slave of the Holy Place, Maksoud of Kashan*. This imposing carpet was almost certainly woven in Tabriz and must have taken fifteen or sixteen years to make, since it would have been commissioned soon after the death of Shah Ismail in 1524. It was discovered in 1892, together with another equally fine carpet. They were both in a very poor state and one was sacrificed in order to repair the other. 36½ feet long, the Ardebil carpet is one of the greatest triumphs of woven art, where the highest artistic feeling for composition and colour combines with sheer technical skill.

Following the Afghan invasions of Persia in the early eighteenth century, Persian carpet weaving was practically abandoned. Under the following Quajar dynasty, Tabriz merchants revived the carpet industry in the 1780s with designs drawn from the Safavid period, and in the nineteenth and early twentieth century many fine carpets were woven, notably those worked in silk at Kashan, Tabriz and Herez.

Ispahan

It is difficult to be certain where the great Safavid carpets were woven for it is not until the seventeenth century that each area developed its own individual style, but as Ispahan was once the capital, it is certain that many carpets were produced in the Court workshops. There is an interesting group of sixteenth- and seventeenth-century carpets, generally called 'Polonaise', which were either made in Ispahan, Tabriz, or possibly Kashan. The silk pile is dyed lime green, yellow, salmon pink and cream, and part of the ground is worked in gold and silver threads, with flowers, palmettes, medallions and cloud bands. The colouring is somewhat similar to the wide sashes worn in Poland, also made of silk and metal thread, many of them signed and dated, and until about 1870, it was thought that the carpets were made in Poland too, possibly by the Madziarski family. This attribution was strengthened by the fact that a number of them bore Polish coats-of-arms. The traveller Tavernier mentions having seen carpets of this description in Persia during the reign of Shah Abbas and it is probable that they found their way to Europe. Perhaps they were presented by Persian Ambassadors at the Polish Court, given by the Shah to visiting envoys, or woven to special order for such families as the Pototskys, Radzivils and the Chartaritskys. Some of the best examples can be seen in the Metropolitan Museum, New York, the Victoria and Albert Museum, London, the Vienna State Museum and the Hermitage in Leningrad. They are not often seen outside museums and one should beware of copies made in Anatolia at the beginning of this century.

About fifty years ago weaving was revived in Ispahan and the small rugs were made with close knotting and good material, the pile being cut very short.

Herat

These rugs are named after the city, now in Afghanistan, which was once part of the Persian province of Khorassan. Fine examples of Herat carpets of the sixteenth and seventeenth century are still to be found and are greatly sought after on account of their rarity. They are long and comparatively narrow and their design has given its name, *herati*, to one of the most popular repetitive patterns found all over the Middle East. The principal colours are brilliant blue, rich red, light green, cream and yellow on an indigo ground. The borders of the antique Herats are worked with flowers, the wide main one carrying a 'turtle' or 'crab' pattern on a yellow ground. Herats are sometimes called Ispahans because of their similarity of design, which can be attributed to the migration of weavers from one district to another. The modern rugs from the area are no longer called Herat, but Kayin.

Joushagan

Joushagan carpets come from a small town in the Kuh-i-Kuru valley, not far away from Kashan. I would date the earliest examples as being seventeenth and eighteenth century, woven with large sprays of flowering shrubs enclosed by a trellis of serrated leaves, the main border bearing a similar 'turtle' pattern to the Herats. The principal colours of these thick heavy carpets are red, blue, yellow and green. Genuine antique Joushagans are rare and command high prices, but even the modern ones are highly regarded. They are woven with the traditional designs in good wool and the colours are still made from vegetable dyes.

Kashan

The city of Kashan was the birthplace of Maksoud, weaver of the Ardebil carpet, and Kashans are perhaps the best known of all Oriental rugs. The seventeenth- and eighteenth-century rugs are rare and expensive as they are finely knotted with the best wool and are dyed in the highest quality vegetable colours in sky blue, jade green, rose, brown and ivory. The field is usually worked with a central medallion with quarter medallions in the spandrels filled with scrolls and flowers, the borders with lotus flowers or blossom. Silk rugs are produced in great quantities and the rich dark blue, pink and green blend together with a faintly metallic lustre. Some of these rugs have the design embossed in silk pile against a flat woven ground.

An antique Oushak *saph* with multiple *mihrabs*

(*overleaf left*) An antique 'Transylvanian' rug
(*overleaf right*) 'Sovereign and Consort Enthroned', Persian, circa 1490,
showing the arrangement of a *kostum* or set of rugs

An antique Persian
'vase' carpet

(*overleaf right*)
A Medjidieh Ghiordes
prayer rug
(*overleaf left*)
An antique 'Basra'
Ghiordes prayer rug

A late 16th century Shah Abbas carpet showing the *herati* design

(*opposite*) Part of an early 16th century Persian carpet

Part of an antique Oushak carpet with the 'Tamerlane' design, cloud bands in the borders

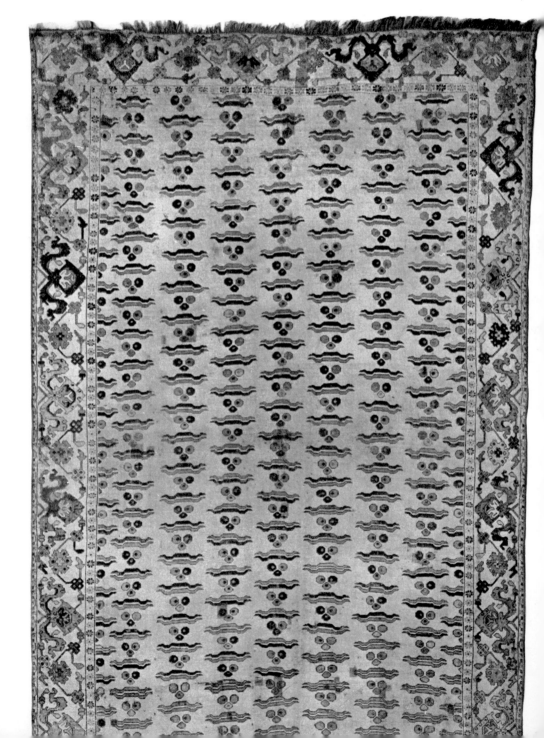

The modern wool Kashan rugs are in no way comparable to those produced even as late as the end of the nineteenth century, as the traditional designs have been copied over and over again until they have become misunderstood and weakened.

Prayer rug designs are used, the field shaped in the form of a *mihrab* and filled with trees and shrubs amongst which are animals and birds. One characteristic of Kashans is the use of blue weft threads, shared only by a few Kermans and Tabriz.

Apart from carpets, Kashan craftsmen make a velvet called Kashan *kadifesi* and delicate silks embroidered in colours with flowers, peacocks and other birds.

Kerman

The province of Kerman is in the south of Persia and has seldom been invaded – except when the Afghans passed through it on their way to Ispahan – so the weavers have been left to make their carpets relatively undisturbed. Since the pastures are good, the wool they get from their sheep is of the best kind, light, soft and durable. The characteristic colours of Kermans are ivory, grey, lime green, pink, brown, indigo and a little light blue, each colour divided from the other by a line of wine red, dark blue or black. The white weft threads are particularly noticeable on the back. As the growing of roses is a local industry, the carpets are filled with these flowers, beautifully executed and shaded. They are often of prayer rug design filled with a 'Tree of Life' as it is called, or worked with a medallion with a pole ending in a lobe projecting from each end. There is a variety of antique Kermans made in Laver, a town near the city of Kerman, with flower-filled fields in beautiful soft colours.

In 1920, when there were many Russian refugees in Turkey, a number of fine Kermans were offered in the Istanbul bazaar, among them some from the collection of Prince Galitzine. My uncle bought them for astronomical prices saying, when we all complained he had overpaid, that nothing was too much for such splendours. They did not remain in his possession for more than a few days before they were sold with a huge profit to the USA. At the end of the nineteenth and during the early twentieth century, Kerman weavers depicted stories from Persian literature or woven portraits of Shahs, Princes and foreign rulers.

Apart from rugs, Kerman is well known for its fine woollen shawls, the best ones being in white wool embroidered in silk. Shawls like these are worn by both men and women among Mohammedans and in the Balkans. They are also used to cover coffins during Moslem funerals.

Sultanabad (Arak)

Carpets started to be made in Sultanabad at some time in the nineteenth century. The older pieces are closely woven with a short pile, but the modern ones are coarse. The design is like that of Mahal with large floral patterns but the knotting is tighter.

Tabriz

Tabriz was under Seljuk rule in the eleventh century, conquered by Ghengis Khan
in the thirteenth and by Tamerlane in the fourteenth, invaded by the Ottoman
Turks in the sixteenth and the Safavids in the seventeenth, and occupied by the
Russians in the nineteenth. It was not until 1925, when the monarch Riza Khan
Pahlavi came to the throne, that the city was restored to peace. Now the capital of
the province of Azerbaidjan, Tabriz is an important place for the carpet industry,
for not only does it produce many rugs of its own, but every day hundreds of
bales of rugs arrive from all over Persia and most local and international companies
are represented in the bazaar. Before the First World War the carpets were very
popular in Russia, Turkey and the Balkans and were sent across the Caspian Sea
to Tiflis or by camel caravan *via* Trebizond to Istanbul. Most of them now go by
air.

The older Tabriz wool carpets, referred to in the market as Jahver Tabriz, are
of medallion design in charming pastel shades of pale rose, green, ivory, orange,
rust red and light blue and they have cartouches in the borders woven with Arabic
quotations. Besides wool carpets, Tabriz is famous for its silk rugs. They are either
of prayer rug design or have fields with a flowering tree or a central medallion.
The silk used is of excellent quality and the colours are rich rust, ivory, pale blue
and orange. The ends of the rugs have long silk fringes.

In 1920 a group of German financiers took over the organisation of the carpet
making in Tabriz and their carpets were called Petag Tabriz, from the initials of
the group – Persische Teppich Aktien Gesellschaft. Today there are a great variety
of rugs made. Although aniline dyes are used, the weaving is good and the rugs
are in demand because of their close knotting and short pile.

Herez

Herez and its neighbouring villages are on the border of Azerbaidjan and the
main occupation of the Iranian Turks who live there is weaving. The district is
well known for its semi-antique silk rugs which are made in all sizes, woven with
a fine Ghiordes knot and the best vegetable dyes. The two principal designs are
similar to those of Tabriz, but the colouring is rather darker and the drawing
bolder. Wool carpets are made with an irregular, somewhat sprawling pattern
of flowers and leaves, the colours being dark and light blue, mustard yellow,
brick red, orange and green.

Gorevan, Mehriban and Sarab (Serapi)

These carpets are woven in the Herez area and are of similar colouring, but the
designs are more angular. There are usually two or three superimposed central

medallions of different colours within a broad main floral border. The weaving is coarse and as the carpets are very thick and heavy, they stand up to a great deal of wear.

Karaja

Karaja is the centre of a group of villages northwest of Herez where two kinds of rugs are woven – Sedjade and Sunnel. Narrow rugs of good quality used to be made, with the *herati* design, but they are rare. The runners being made now with medallion designs in madder red, indigo blue and white are of poor quality.

Bahsheish

Long narrow rugs used to be made in the early nineteenth century with close knotting and shiny wool, but those made now are very coarse. The designs are similar to those of Mehriba.

Arak

Arak is the capital of the province in Central Persia of the same name and is the market for the rugs of the surrounding area, all woven with the Senne knot, such as Mahal, Muskabad, Sarouk, Fereghan and Sarabend.

Mahal

Named after the district of Mahal, these large carpets woven by nomads are loosely knotted and are of poor design, being perhaps the lowest grade of all Persian fabrics. Medallion designs are common and repetitive floral patterns are also used in dark blue, red, white, black and ivory. Many of them are sold to Germany, Switzerland and Scandinavia and it is probable that they are appreciated because of their strong colours and heavy, thick pile.

Muskabad

Muskabad is a town in Arak province. The carpets are of large size and coarse weaving, cotton being used for the warp and weft.

Sarouk

Sarouk rugs are named after a small town in the Fereghan plain. I do not know when weaving started there, but they first came to the Istanbul bazaar in the late nineteenth century. They have excellent vegetable dyes and very fine knotting. The medallion, floral and animal designs are well drawn and sharply defined by a dark line around each patch of colour. The short pile is closely clipped and dyed ivory, dark blue, brown, a bright, hot red and a soft green. Sarouks are very attractive for, although they are tightly woven, they always lie straight on the floor without curling at the edges.

Feraghan

These rugs are named after a district in Central Persia. They are woven in all sizes with the *herati* design of flowerheads and curving leaves or with the Gulli Henna design of sprigs of white henna flowers. The antiques are called Mostafi Feraghans and are easily recognised by the characteristic lime green of the main border, which has usually worn lower than the remainder of the pile, leaving the border design of lotus flowers in relief. The field is dark blue or red with the pattern in dark and light blue with touches of yellow, apricot and green. Today the work is of no importance as the carpets are coarsely woven with cheap dyes.

Zilli-Sultan

These rugs are named after a much admired governor of Feraghan province called Zilli-Sultan Khan and are of the very best quality. So tightly are they knotted that they were surely made by young girls, but because of this very quality the foundation threads often break and the delicate rugs must be treated with great care. The colours are usually bright red, green and black on a jade green or ivory ground, and the field is worked with a repetitive design either of small bunches of flowers in vases flanked on each side by a bird, or else cypress trees and birds, so minute in detail that they seem to be painted rather than woven. The rugs today are rare and expensive.

Sarabend

The best rugs are called Mir-Sarabends. It is not certain how they came by their name. There is a village called Miriabad in the Sarabend district, but I was told once that they were named in honour of a famous chief (*mir*), Mir Ahmed Seyyid Aga, in the early nineteenth century, The dark blue or red ground is woven with rows of palmettes or cones and the main border, which is ivory or pink, has a continuous design of vine leaves and cones, edged with six or seven narrow stripes. The rarest form of Sarabend is a set of four pieces, a *Kostum*. Two of the rugs (*yans*) are long and narrow where the guests are seated according to their rank, the children being put at the far end. The middle one serves as a table for food, and the top one (*kelleyi*) is for the head of the family and guests of honour.

The modern Sarabends are poor quality runners or rugs with a coarse Turkish knot and aniline dyes in red, blue and white.

An Ispahan rug with a 'Tree of Life'

Detail of an antique Herat carpet with the *herati* design

A Kashan rug, the field of *mihrab* design

A Kashan silk carpet with a pole medallion in the field and a palmette border

A Fereghan rug

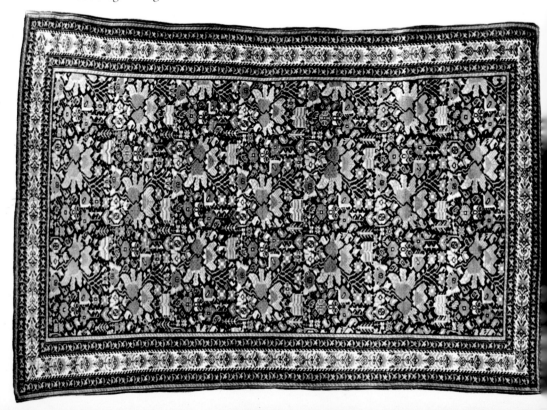

A pictorial Ispahan rug with a *mihrab*-shaped field

A rare Shiraz rug of prayer-rug form woven by the nomadic Kashkai tribe

An antique Khorassan carpet

An antique 'star' Oushak carpet

Kurdistan

The nomadic Kurdish tribes have settled in Turkey, Iraq, Azerbaidjan and in the mountains of western Persia – Kurdistan. They mostly belong to the Sunni sect of Islam, speak their own language, regardless of which country they now live in, and until recently, were governed by their own chiefs. Despite their rebellious, warlike character, they are a gay and hospitable people. It is the Persian Kurds still living in feudal conditions in the mountains who show the greatest ability in weaving such carpets as Bijar, Senne, Hamadan, and Malayer. They rarely change their designs but are content to go on weaving in the same way year after year.

A notable group of carpets come from this area which go under the general name of Kurdistan. They are woven with the Minna Khani design – stylised flowerheads and scrolls forming a trellis – with a thick pile, partly in goat and camel hair. The carpets end in strips of kelim weaving which have coloured lines running through it. The vegetable dyes are dark blue, cream, rose, yellow, green, a little black and dark brown.

Bijar

The name Bijar is taken from a town northwest of Hamadan. Carpets or small rugs are made with a double knot and are so firmly woven that they are heavy and stiff. It is almost impossible to fold them and they have to be rolled. The lustrous wool is of good quality and the vegetable dyes give rich brilliant red, dark blue, ivory and green. A large amount of natural, undyed camel hair is used. The field is often left completely undecorated, except for an *abrash* (variation in colour) across its width, and a central medallion filled with the *herati* design. Antiques are rare and although those sixty to seventy years old are good, the modern productions are of poor quality.

Senne

Sennes are very tightly knotted, the pile being clipped right down until it feels almost bristly to the touch, and almost invariably have a diamond-shaped central medallion and spandrels filled with the *herati* design on a small scale. The colours are dark and light blue, pink, and green. The knotting on the back has a speckled look unlike any other rug.

Senne Kelim

There are a number of Senne *kelims* to be found, their design and colouring similar to the pile rugs, but the effect of the flat diagonal weaving is like *moiré* silk.

(*opposite above*) Detail of the borders of a 'Transylvanian' rug showing how the lozenge pattern is bisected at the corners
(*opposite below*) A Kiz-Ghiordes rug

Hamadan

Hamadan, the ancient city of Ekbatana, is situated on the foothills of Mount Alvand. Arabs and Turks live in Hamadan besides Persians and indeed Turkish is mostly spoken and the weavers use the Ghiordes knot. The rugs and runners are notable for the large amount of camel hair in the pile, shaded from dark to light brown, but the other colours used are synthetic. The weaving is coarse and the designs often imitate Caucasian rugs. The older runners, which were woven in the nineteenth century, usually have medallions connected to each other by a pole on a plain camel hair ground. The borders are again left plain except for a few scattered human figures or animals.

There is a certain type of long rug called Mosul-Hamadan which has a diagonal pattern of cones or stripes in the field. Since Mosul is in Iraq and Hamadan is in Persia, the only possible reason why they have this name is that the rugs from Hamadan were once shipped to Turkey *via* Mosul.

Besides the rugs woven in Hamadan itself, all those made by the Kurdish tribes as well as the surrounding districts and villages are sold in the Hamadan bazaar.

Malayer

Almost all Malayer rugs are woven under Hamadan influence, but the Senne knot is used and the work is of better quality.

Shiraz

These rugs are woven mainly by tribes of Turkish and Fars origin and are named after the city of Shiraz, which apart from its carpet industry is rich in rice, cotton, tobacco, opium and cattle, the main export being *karakul* or lambskin.

Although they are not highly regarded, all Shiraz rugs are made from good soft wool and vegetable dyes in rich shades of ruby red, dark blue, yellow, white and ivory. They are easily distinguishable by the multi-coloured overbinding at the sides of the rugs, a characteristic shared by Niris.

The best quality Shiraz are called 'laver Shiraz' and are a hundred years old or more. The others are not more than fifty. Their wool has an exceptional sheen and they have an all-over design of roses. They are woven with a double knot with pieces of embroidered *kelim* at each end. The other grades of Shiraz are called Kurdish, Kashkai and Mecca. The first two are woven by the Kashkai tribes, who live in their black tents or *yurts* in the valleys and plains around Shiraz, the former grade being loosely woven with long pile. The Mecca rugs are so named because most of them are sold in the markets of Mecca, to which hundreds of thousands of Moslems make a pilgrimage each year. They have diamond-shaped medallions surrounded by scattered figures, animals and jewellery.

Niriz

These rugs are woven by nomadic tribes near lake Niriz and have large cones in the field in green, apricot and red on a dark blue ground. One border is often filled with carnations, another with stripes like a barber's pole. The edges are overbound in parti-coloured wool.

Afshar

The nomadic tribe of Afshar still make vegetable dyes, and the wool of the particular type of sheep they herd is soft and lustrous. Of small size, Afshars are considered to be a poor grade of Shiraz, to which they bear some resemblance. The designs are simple in conception, consisting mainly of flowers scattered throughout the field, within narrow borders, in red, yellow, white and cream, blue being the predominant colour. There is often an *abrash* and the rugs themselves are irregular and lie badly on the floor.

Yezd

Yezd, the ancient city of Yezda, lies between Kerman and Nain and has a good reputation for its silk jewellery and gold. Even though they have only been made since the beginning of this century, the rugs are well thought of because they are closely knotted and have beautiful designs in soft colours. They bear such a close resemblance to old Kermans that it is sometimes difficult to tell them apart. The design of a central medallion and four spandrels is worked with a Senne knot, and the short pile is dyed pastel green, rose, light blue and ivory. Hardly any have been exported and they remain in mosques and in the houses of well-off Persians.

Tehran

Until recently, rug weaving has been neglected in Tehran, the capital of Iran, although the city was known as the centre of the wholesale and retail trade. Even though the rugs are modern, they surpass many others with their fine knotting, closely-cut pile and good dyes. They are woven in the traditional designs of the sixteenth and seventeenth centuries and the best examples are knotted by young orphans under royal patronage. The ground colour is usually brick red or blue, and the patterns are in light and dark blue, green and white.

Nain

The small provincial town of Nain, near Yezd, was once a fortress, Although weaving only began there in about 1920, when the rugs were first sold in the

Istanbul bazaar, they were immediately accepted as being the highest quality modern Iranian work. The closely knotted, dense pile is made from the best wool and dyes and has either a floral medallion or the Shah Abbas design in red, blue, black and yellow on a white ground, sometimes with a small quantity of silk.

Qum

These rugs from the city of Qum are next only to Nain in quality among the modern productions. Generally woven in wool, they are sometimes in silk or a mixture of the two, and are worked with a hunting scene or vases of flowers and birds of paradise in a light celadon green, white, turquoise and rose.

Baktiari

Named after the nomadic tribe who live near Ispahan, these rugs are very popular in Germany and Switzerland owing to their bright colouring and original designs. Vegetable dyes and good quality wool are used and the warp is usually cotton (although goat hair is sometimes found). These rugs, which can be bought cheaply in every market, are extremely durable. Baktiaris are made in all sizes and the field either has a central medallion or it is divided into many squares enclosing flowers, trees and miniature prayer rugs. Large areas of yellow are used with white, dark brown, orange, red and bright blue.

Meshed

Meshed is the capital of the province of Khorassan, which lies on the route along which invaders from the East have come. In it lies the tomb of the eighth Imam Riza, and the city is considered sacred to the Sh'ia sect. Throughout the year thousands of pilgrims from all parts of Islam visit the city and afterwards take the title of Meshedi. Although not of very good quality, the older Mesheds have vegetable dyes which are quite sound. Aniline dyes are used in the modern ones, the colours being washed in acid after weaving to tone down some of their rawness and to give the impression that the rugs are older than they seem. Together with the Khorassan rugs, Mesheds have a distinctive weave. Although either the Turkish or Persian knot is used, every now and then the knots are tied on four warp threads rather than two, which causes thick raised lines on the back, and wherever the rug is worn, tufts of foundation threads can be seen from the front. Both carpets and small rugs are made, the central medallion and spandrels being filled with flowers. The principal colours used are magenta and blue, with a little yellow, green and ivory.

(*opposite*) An antique Mezarlik Kulab rug

Borders of 17th, 18th and 19th century prayer rugs

(*opposite*) A rare antique Ghiordes rug

(*overleaf* Two prayer rugs made at the Top-Kapi Serai in Istanbul

An antique Kula prayer rug with a tchoubouclu border

An antique Ladik prayer rug with an inscription in the *mihrab*

A Mudjur prayer rug with the rare feature of a double *mihrab*

(*overleaf left*) A prayer rug made at the Top-Kapi Serai in Istanbul

Khurassan

The finest and oldest specimens that were made in this huge province are called Khurassans, although I believe them to have been woven in Meshed itself. Dating from the second half of the eighteenth century, these antiques are generally long and narrow carpets in velvet red, green, a little yellow and indigo blue. One of the rarest designs is a plain field overlaid with an elongated central medallion. Another has flowers all over the field, the corners each with a large vase supported by two swans, within twelve or more narrow borders. In another variety of these attractive carpets, the field and narrow border have multi-coloured vertical stripes which are woven with vine leaves, flowers and – a feature peculiar to Khurassans – a small cone laid on top of a larger one. Many of the antique Khurassans are signed and dated.

Gayin (Qain)

Gayin rugs have colourful pastel rose and pistachio green repetitive patterns, similar to the Herat rugs of the eighteenth century. The Senne knot is used and the rugs come in all sizes.

3

turkey

The Seljuks

Knotted rugs were probably introduced into western Asia by the Seljuks who established themselves there in the eighth and ninth centuries. Originally from Transcaspia, these Turkish tribes then migrated to Persia and gained more and more strength and power until they finally took control in the middle of the seventh century. By 1078 they had conquered Anatolia, having fought a decisive battle with the Byzantines, and established Konya as the capital of their Empire under Sultan Masud 1 (1116-56).

While the Seljuks of Iran were already being crushed by the invading armies of Ghengis Khan, the Turkish Seljuk culture was reaching its highest peak in the mid-thirteenth century, influenced not only by the Byzantines, but by direct contact with the art of the East. Persians, Jews, Turkomans, Tartars, Syrians, Kurds, Bulgarians and Arabs all lived together, and Christian Armenians and Greeks worked side by side with Moslem craftsmen. Marco Polo, visiting Konya in 1283, wrote that he had seen the most exquisite hand-knotted rugs with beautiful

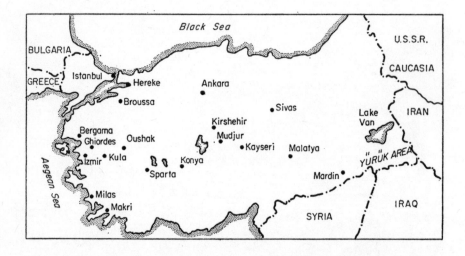

colours and original motifs, and the Arab traveller, Ibn Battuta, writing fifty years later, thought that the Turkish carpets were the best in the world.

The few fragments of Seljuk rugs that survive show a highly developed art with a simple repeating design in the field and broad borders with patterns based on Kufic, the early Arabic writing, lozenges and stars. Their colours are striking and effective – yellow, red, green, dark blue and white.

The Ottomans

Towards the end of the thirteenth century, the power of the Seljuks in Turkey declined and the country was ruled by a number of small local dynasties, one of these, the Osmanlis, finally taking control. They first appeared in Anatolia as the Kayi tribe from the Mongolian steppes with their leader Süleyman Shah and his son Ertughrul Gazi. In return for helping the Seljuks in one of their many battles, they received a small principality. After the death of Ertughrul in 1281, his son Osman and his men gave the Seljuks further aid and were allowed by Sultan Masud to create their own independent state. The tribe had elected Osman as their leader or *ghazi* ('Fighter for the Faith') and he gave his name to the new dynasty – Ottoman, derived from the Arabic form of his name, Othman.

Osman's successor, Sultan Orkhan Gazi (1324-62) captured Bursa (Broussa) and Isnik (Nicaea) from the Byzantines, and from then on the Ottoman Empire grew until most of western Islam was subjugate. By 1400 they were strong enough to be little affected by the invasions of the savage conqueror, Timur (Tamerlane) from Samarkand and in 1453 the great Byzantine city of Constantinople was besieged, overcome and occupied by Sultan Mehmed II Fatih.

Although cruel and pitiless despots, Sultan Selim, the Grim (1470-1520) and his son, Sultan Süleyman, the Magnificent (1520-66), shared a love and admiration

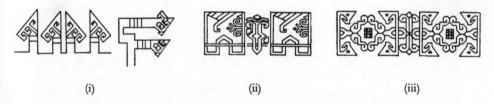

(i)   (ii)   (iii)

Stylised Kufic lettering in the border of (i) a 13th Century Seljuk carpet, (ii) a 17th Century Oushak carpet and (iii) a 19th Century Shirvan rug

of the arts and by offering large sums of money, high rank and honours, persuaded the artisans to set aside all the old motifs and to develop a new, independent Turkish style. The best artists and craftsmen were drawn from all over the vast Empire which, by the end of Süleyman's reign, stretched from Hungary and Egypt to Persia in the East. These men brought new ideas into Turkey, already producing the highest quality silks, velvets, pottery, calligraphy and painting.

Weaving under the Ottomans

As the Turks belong to the Sunni sect of Moslems, mostly prayer rugs were made, although as a result of extensive trade with Europe, other rugs and carpets were woven for the export market with stylised flowers, strapwork and leaves, or large medallions. In the eighteenth and nineteenth centuries, new weaving centres grew up, such as Melas, Mudjur, Megri and Yuruk, while in the already existing rugs of Ladik, Ghiordes, Bergama and Koula, flowers assumed greater importance. It was during the reign of Ahmed III (1703-30) that the 'tulip period' (*lale deviri*)

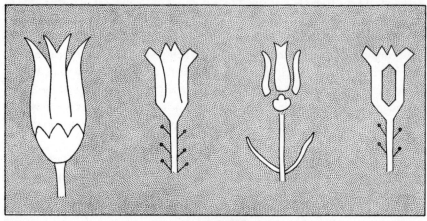

TULIPS

reached its height. Most of the Sultans had interested themselves in the gardens of their palace, Top-Kapi Serai, known as the Seraglio, and had imported roses, hyacinths, lilacs, carnations and ranaculus. But it was the tulip above all that was loved by Ahmed and he even created the office of Master of Flowers in

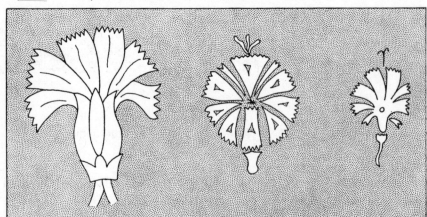

CARNATIONS

order to protect them. In 1562 an Amsterdam merchant first brought tulip bulbs from Istanbul to Holland; in the next century an Austrian ambassador in Turkey reintroduced the improved flower from Holland. Tulip fêtes were held during

An antique Bergama rug

(*above left*) A fighting dragon and phoenix in a 17th century kelim carpet (detail)

(*above right*) The same motif in an Armenian Kouba (detail)

The mark of the Royal Hereke looms

A Megri prayer rug

A Shirvan rug

the nights of the full moon and it was one of the Sultan's greatest pleasures to watch dwarfs with candles on their heads wandering among hundreds of these flowers, each with a tiny lamp of coloured glass in its centre, and cages of singing birds.

The later Ottoman period

I shall call this period of Turkish art *tanzimat deviri* or rococo, as it came under a strong influence of Western culture, particularly that of France. The rugs are Kizil and Medjidieh Ghiordes, Kirshehir, Banderma, Hereke, Feshane, Sivas, Kendirli Koula and Broussa. Although the rugs of the first part of this period are of no particular artistic merit, exceptional silk rugs in imitation of earlier styles were made around the turn of this century, notably those from the royal looms of Hereke, while in his little factory in Constantinople, or Istanbul as it was called by the Turks, an old Armenian master weaver, Zare-Aga, created some magnificent pieces. Apart from the large heavily-knotted wool carpets from Sparta, Demirji and Borlu, there are many rugs named after the towns and villages where they are woven, such as Chanak-Kale, Yagdju-Bedir, Yahyali and Nigde, mostly unknown names, as the rugs are sold in mixed lots in the Istanbul bazaar to wholesalers who classify them into groups and only a local expert can identify each one correctly. The older pieces are bought by Turkish dealers and the remainder are exported in bulk all over the world.

Konya

Konya, once the capital of the Seljuk Empire and home of the Whirling Dervishes, was famous as a weaving centre from the twelfth century to the eighteenth. A number of rugs from the Seljuk period were found not very long ago still in use in the Alâ ed-dîn Mosque in Konya. These were worked with geometric patterns, dragons and other animals which show a strong Chinese and Mongolian influence. The main colours of this early period were red, blue, green and white and the best examples are to be found only in Museums, the Islamic Art Museum in Istanbul having one of the richest collections. Later, prayer rugs were woven and a golden yellow was added to the colours.

Oushak

Oushaks were one of the most exported carpets in the sixteenth and seventeenth centuries and were to be found on the altars of European churches and in the houses of the rich. Many were woven to order and bear the coats-of-arms of such famous names as Count Stroganoff, Cardinal Wolsey, Baron Orsini, Count Esterhazi and Prince Cantacuzene. At first they were made in small sizes and were designed either with stylised birds on a white ground ('bird' Oushaks) or interlaced strapwork in yellow and red with touches of green, blue and white ('Holbein'

Oushaks). Both these and the large and impressive 'star' Oushaks, with their shaped medallions and loose weaving in brick red and blue, were painted not only by Holbein, but by Lotto, Memling, Zurbarán, Vermeer and many others. Other rugs were woven with three small circles above two wavy lines arranged in groups all over the field. We are told that the Mongol, Tamerlane ordered this design, symbolic of his sovereignty over three parts of the world, to be displayed in every city he had conquered.

Occasionally one comes across *saphs* which have two or three rows of *mihrabs*.

'Transylvanian'

These rugs are of Turkish origin, probably from Koula and not as is thought from Ladik, Oushak or Bergama and certainly not from Rumania and Hungary, where they were found. In the sixteenth century, Sultan Süleyman invaded Transylvania, and in order to show the West that the victorious army and their leader were not barbarians, Kara Ahmet Pasha, the military commander, gave on behalf of the Sultan a beautiful rug for the altar of the Black Church in Brasov as a gesture of goodwill and respect towards Christianity. His magnanimity won prestige and as a result an order was placed by the Patriarch for as many as two thousand rugs, which were distributed to all the churches in Rumania and Hungary. Merchants were quick to import more of these attractive rugs and others were given to the churches in thanksgiving for the safe journey between Turkey and Transylvania.

Of small size, the rugs have a floral design in the central medallion and corners and have a broad border with a lozenge pattern or large flowerheads flanked by two formal leaves from which spring two hyacinths. The colours are strawberry red, light blue, yellow and cream. Other rugs were ordered for secular use and these were of prayer rug design, either with a plain *mihrab* or four columns supporting the niche. In antique rugs of this kind, the scale of the design remains the same even if a smaller rug is woven, which results in the corners of the border being cut off, so that the two halves of a vertical and horizontal lozenge butt against each other. An unusual feature of 'Transylvanians' is a strip of *kelim* weaving at either end, found more often in Transcaspian than Turkish work. Unfortunately the rugs became very worn in the houses, although those found in the churches were in an excellent state of preservation. Western artists were fond of them and they can be seen in many paintings of the Italian, Dutch and German schools. Today, it is difficult to discover 'Transylvanians' outside museums and they are sold for high prices when they do appear.

Ghiordes

These famous rugs are named after Ghiordes, the ancient city of Gordium, in the district of Smyrna, and are separated into several different groups:

BASRA GHIORDES: The best customers for fine rugs were to be found in the Arab market of Basra, to which this type of Ghiordes was sent. They are the largest of all Turkish prayer rugs and like Ladiks, have a very short pile. From the centre of the arch hangs a mosque lamp on the otherwise plain *mihrab*, which is usually ivory or dark blue and above and below there is a rectangular cross panel. The borders are richly decorated with carnations or lotus in rose, blue, green and ivory.

It can be seen that the borders of antique Ghiordes are similar to the floral border of the 'Transylvanian' rugs, but the flowers during the course of time have become smaller and more cramped, losing some of the simplicity and dignity of the earlier work.

KIZ-GHIORDES: These are smaller than other Ghiordes and were woven by young girls, either for their dowry or to be sent to the harems of the Sultan and Grand Pasha for use as prayer rugs by the wives and concubines. Finely knotted with delicate designs of flowers within borders of zig-zags, they are in pastel shades of ivory, rose, jade green and turquoise blue.

TCHOUBOUCLU (SHOBOKLI) GHIORDES: These are another type of prayer rug of the seventeenth and eighteenth centuries with blue *mihrabs*, the borders composed of many long, narrow, stick-like stripes in black and white.

SINEKLI: The *mihrabs* of these prayer rugs are entirely covered with a stylised representation of flies (*sineklis*) against a ground of rich velvety red or blue. They are extremely rare so it is not surprising that they are valuable. Several specimens can be seen in the Evkaf Museum in Istanbul and in the Cairo Museum.

MEDJIDIEH AND KIZIL GHIORDES: These are two examples of Ghiordes weaving that are not highly regarded by connoisseurs and consequently can be bought at a much lower figure. They were made during the reign of Sultan Abd-el-Medjid (1839-61) at a time when a taste for French rococo furniture swept through Turkey in place of native styles. In order to carry through the theme in the salons of the palace, the Sultan dictated that the Ghiordes weavers should use the French Savonnerie designs against a background of bright red, *kizil* being the Turkish word for this colour.

Apart from these last two types, antique Ghiordes rugs are usually in their original condition for two reasons. Firstly, prayer rugs are invariably rolled up and placed in a coffer or chest after use until they are needed again and secondly, most of the Ghiordes in Oriental collections are hung on a wall. All antique Ghiordes rugs should really be hung and not placed on the floor, as they are masterpieces of Turkish weaving and should be preserved for posterity.

Kula

Named after the city of Kula near Smyrna, an important centre of weaving in the seventeenth and eighteenth centuries. Sometimes confused with Ghiordes, they are divided into various categories:

DIREKLI KULA: The *mihrab* of these prayer rugs is surmounted by a single rect-angular panel often filled with s-shapes resembling salamanders, one of the symbols of the ancient fire-worshipping Zoroastrian religion. The lower corners of the niche are supported by floral columns and the colours are indigo blue, buff and pink.

MEZARLIK KULA: Here *mezarlik* means tomb, although the exact translation of the word is cemetery. These very unusual rugs were made to cover the tombs of Sultans, of their families and members of the nobility. The *mihrab* has a break in it to symbolise the entrance into Paradise and is filled with rows of cypress trees and tombs. They have an odd number of borders as the weavers consider this a talis-man against the Evil Eye and their extremely agreeable colours are cherry red, sky blue, yellow and light green. Some of the finest examples are to be seen in the crypt at Broussa covering the tombs of Seljuk and Ottoman Sultans, woven with the Arabic inscription: *Salaam Aleikum – Wa Ramatullah* ('Rest in Peace – in God's Mercy').

KOMURJU KULA: First made in the eighteenth century, they are called 'coal' Kulas because of the large amount of natural black goat's hair in the pile. With their silky texture and dark colour scheme of black, brick red and *patlijani* (aubergine), these rugs have a rich and luxurious appearance. The *mihrab* has a stylised flowering tree with an inscription above. Komurju Kulas can be found in good rug shops and are not too expensive by comparison with other types. Although they are still made, the modern pieces are so inferior to the older ones as not to merit serious attention.

KINDIRLY KULA: These small rugs were knotted at the end of the eighteenth century with the warp and weft of flax. Thought by local collectors to be good examples of primitive art, they were coarsely knotted, their high pile being coloured yellow, indigo and ivory.

Ladik

The name Ladik originates from the Greek Lazikiya, Latakia or Laodicea, but it is a mystery where these famous rugs were actually woven. Although there are still a number of towns and villages called Ladik in Asia Minor, there is no reason to believe that any of them were rug centres. Most of them are too small even to appear on the map and the only Ladik officially mentioned, a town in the province of Amasya, shows no sign of ever having had a tradition of weaving. The only place where weaving does seem to have actually taken place is in the tiny village of Ladik in the district of Saray-Onu, about forty kilometres north of Konya where, according to the Islamic Encyclopaedia, the principal occupation in the nineteenth century was making rugs as well as coarse woollen cloths and quilted covers. Whether the Ladik rugs were ever woven in that village, is not certain, but there is no doubt that they bear a strong resemblance to Konyas in design, colour and even in texture and it is possible that Ladik craftsmen went to work in Konya or vice versa.

Ladik prayer rugs are different from others. The *mihrab* has a triple arch, the central one being the highest, and each is supported by two slender columns. The spandrels of the seventeenth-century pieces are usually filled with giant leaves while the eighteenth-century rugs have a large panel above or below the *mihrab* woven with a row of angular tulips. The most usual borders have tulips set obliquely across them, alternating with large flowerheads. The best Ladiks have a splendid velvet red or blue *mihrab* and there are a few with a white ground which are owned by the Islamic Museum in Istanbul and the Metropolitan Museum in New York. There is a still rarer type which has a *kitabe* or inscription on the white ground. Indeed, the only one I know of in existance is in the collection of my wife. Such a valuable piece must surely have been made for the Sultan himself. The *kitabe* reads 'Religious devotion is your destiny. Death will bring an end to patient suffering.' Other colours used besides blue and red are emerald green, cream and sometimes a canary yellow and are of such richness that they glow like jewels.

Genuine antique Ladiks are not often found and when they are, they command high prices, especially in the United States where they are in great demand among collectors. The modern Ladiks are plentiful and can be bought for a modest sum.

Istanbul

Recently some very fine wool and silk rugs were discovered in the vaults beneath the harem of the Top-Kapi Serai. As a member of the Top-Kapi Museum Society, I was given permission to photograph these pieces, and after a long and careful examination with Mr A. Kent and Mr V. Yakoubian, we came to the following conclusions: these marvellous, beautiful and rare pieces were made some time in the seventeenth, eighteenth and nineteenth centuries. They have extremely close knotting, with about four hundred knots to the square inch – or 57,600 to the square foot. A prayer rug of fifteen square feet would take one girl several years to make. Because of the labour involved, the superb quality of the material and the Persian feeling of the designs, the rugs were presumably made by Persian concubines. It is probable that the young girl would present the rug to the Queen

Mother (*Sultan Validé*) or to the Chief Eunuch of the harem (*Kizlar Agha*), both of whom had enormous influence over the Sultan, in order to gain their sympathy and protection, and in the hope that one day the rug might reach the Sultan himself and attract his attention. A number of the rugs are *namazliks* with quotations from the Koran, their colours in dark red, blue, green, *café-au-lait* and white. At present only a few of the rugs are exhibited in the Museum, where visitors can see them.

Bergama

The rugs from Bergama, the ancient Greek city of Pergamum, are of a very distinctive type, being close to Caucasian rugs in their rich colouring and geometric designs. They are highly decorative and their deep pile and close weave make them popular in the East as well as in the West. The best examples are eighteenth century prayer rugs called Sandikli Bergamas, which are larger than the others and have a strip of *kelim* weaving at either end. Generally Bergamas are almost square and are dyed red, blue and white, the predominant colour in the Sandiklis being orange.

Mudjur

Named after the city of Mudjur in the south of Turkey, these nineteenth-century rugs are renowned for their bright orange, red, yellow and green colouring which has a pleasing and cheerful effect. The prayer rugs usually have stepped *mihrabs* in plain colours but the older and more prized pieces have a double *mihrab* and there are also a number of *saphs*. The borders always have stylised flowers forming squares, and the weft threads are often dyed red.

Milas

Up to the end of the eighteenth century, no rugs were known to have been made in Milas, on the shore of the Aegean Sea, but by the beginning of the nineteenth century there were a great many being woven by the villagers, who were of Greek origin. The loosely-woven prayer rugs are of small size, with either a diamond-shaped niche or two narrow *mihrabs* filled with carnations. The colouring is brown, white, light blue, rose and yellow and the warp and weft threads are often dyed yellow or red. The early Milas rugs are very popular in Germany and the USA.

Megri (Makri)

Megri is a little place not far away from Milas, but the weavers have developed a highly original design for their prayer rugs with two narrow *mihrabs* in different colours surrounded by broad borders of carnations. Dating from the same period as Melas, the material and dyes are of good quality. The colours are blue, brown and green, with occasional touches of red and white.

Yuruk

Their name means 'wanderer' and they are woven by a nomadic Kurdish tribe living on the western side of Kurdistan, which runs between Asia Minor and Persia. They are mostly about a hundred years old, woven from good quality wool which gives a silken lustre to the pile. Although not highly regarded because of their coarse weave and tendency to lose their shape, they are nevertheless interesting because of their primitive designs. Prayer rugs are found with roughly shaped *mihrabs*, but the rugs are generally long and narrow.

Kirsehir

Named after the small Anatolian city, Kirshehir rugs are semi-antiques. They follow the design of Koula tomb rugs and are noted for their beautiful shades of green and rose. Strangely enough, they are neither collected in Turkey nor sold to the West.

Panderma

Master weavers of Armenian origin established their workshops in the nineteenth century around Panderma on the shore of the Sea of Marmara and began to make prayer rugs of Ghiordes or Kula design, very finely knotted in soft pastel colours. No one paid any attention to these until after the First World War, when Western dealers as well as local traders began to appreciate them and a large quantity were sent all over the world. Before the Second World War had begun, however, the Panderma weavers had stopped making them.

Kayseri

Named after the city which, after 1920, became a centre for the manufacture of standard export rugs, Kayseris were woven in imitation of Persian and Turkish designs in all sizes from small mats up to large carpets, in wool as well as in silk and artificial silk. The rugs of Kayseri are mainly exported or sold in the Istanbul Grand Bazaar to tourists.

Sparta

Sparta is really a misnomer for the city of Isbarta in the southwest of Asia Minor and has nothing to do with the city in Greece. They are modern and have no original designs of their own, copying Persian or Chinese models. Both rugs and large carpets are woven with a coarse knot, and the thick pile is heavy and hardwearing. The most typical colouring is blue, green and rose pink and the ground is often ivory, although other colours such as mauve and ochre are used when a 'Chinese' carpet is being made.

Hereke

This little town in northern Turkey became famous around the end of the nineteenth century when silk carpets were produced under the patronage of Sultan Abdul Hamid. Many of the designs are in the Persian style with animal forms, flowers and scrollwork or with the tall curving *mihrab* of the antique Persian prayer rug. Others were of Western inspiration. They themselves were copied in the 1930s in Corfu under the direction of the weaver Tossounian, but true Herekes have a small mark or signature in the border. They are so finely woven in silk or wool, with inscriptions in gold or silver thread, that the Sultan considered them suitable for him to offer to royal visitors as presents on their departure. Among the distinguished guests to receive these magnificent rugs were Queen Victoria of England, the Empress Eugenie of France, the Russian Tsar Alexander III and the German Emperor Wilhelm. In 1922 when all the members of the reigning Turkish royal family left the country to live in exile abroad, a great number of Herekes were sold by auction, most of them passing into the hands of American dealers who sold them to private collectors.

Kum-Kapu

At the beginning of this century, the Armenian weavers of Kum-Kapu began to make silk rugs. The first ones appeared in the workshop of the master weaver Zare-Aga and quickly earned a high reputation and became much sought after, especially those monogrammed by the master himself. They were knotted in silk with gold and silver threads and copied antique Persian prayer rug, hunting or animal designs. Today they are rare and expensive.

Sivas

This Anatolian town, as well as the surrounding province, has a reputation for good quality rugs of all sizes. They first appeared at the beginning of the nineteenth century, copying the Tabriz rugs with all-over floral patterns or central medallions and similar spandrels. The best quality wool and vegetable dyes are still used in the rugs and the rose, jade-green, blue, ivory and cream colouring is both delicate and pleasing.

(*opposite*) A Kazak rug

A Surahani rug

(*opposite*) A Hile rug

Feshane

The royal factory founded by Sultan Medjid in the nineteenth century is in the Eyub district of Istanbul. Feshane made large carpets of French Aubusson and Savonnerie designs in pastel shades and earned popularity among the Turkish and Egyptian nobility, to whom most of them were exported. Today, the looms produce cloth in place of carpets.

Broussa

The first capital of the young Ottoman Empire, Broussa, was once famous for superb velvets and silks. As the centre of the silk industry, Broussa produced only silk rugs, the earliest being made during the last years of the nineteenth century. They were finely woven, copying Turkish prayer rugs or sixteenth and seventeenth century Persian rugs, and are found with a variety of colours including ivory, cream, rose, scarlet, green and sky blue, sometimes with metallic thread.

Demirji

Named after a little village, these 'Turkey' carpets, as they were widely known, are of inferior quality and very coarse weave, but were to be found in every house of Victorian England. Their colouring is mainly dark red, blue and green and they have sprawling patterns of flowers and leaves.

Borlu

Until the last few years no attention was given to these carpets, but because of their pastel colours, they suddenly gained favour in the USA and are now in demand. The earliest pieces are not more than forty to fifty years old and are made in large carpet sizes with medium grain knots and light colours, mostly from vegetable dyes.

Kelims

The cheapest quality pileless rugs in Turkey are known as *ketchi* and are woven with goat hair. The second grade are *kelim* and the third and best are *kiz-kelim*, woven by young girls as part of their dowry and used for bridal bed covers. The finest ones are worked with silver and gold threads.

(*opposite*) A Chichi rug

4

Caucasia and Armenia

Caucasia is that part of Russia which forms an isthmus stretching between the Caspian and the Black Sea, joining both Turkey and Persia. The population totals about seven million and is composed of five different races of very mixed origin, Mohammedan Turks, Gregorian Armenians, Jews and Orthodox Georgians and Russians. A wild land with great mountains, Caucasia until the nineteenth century was never a single state, but was occupied and reoccupied many times by successive armies. The Armenians and Georgians were ruled by their own kinds and the Turkish areas were divided into small principalities or *hanliks*. By 1822 Tsar Alexander I had conquered all the *hanliks* except Daghestan, until finally in 1859, after more than thirty years' guerilla warfare, the Turkish leader Imam Shamil gave up the fight against the army of the Tsar's general, Prince Baratinsky. Imam Shamil was brought to St Petersburg. There, Alexander refused to accept the surrender of his sabre out of respect for Imam Shamil's courage and he allowed him and his men to go free.

On 6 September 1859 the Russian campaign ended and all of Caucasia became part of the Russian Empire until 1918, when the Turkish army under the command

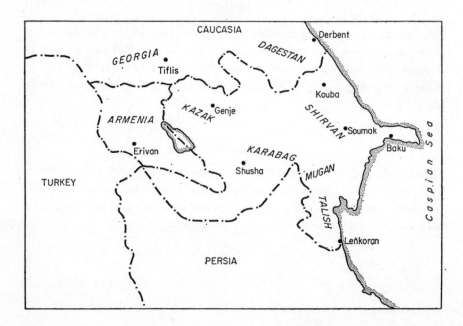

of Mursel and Nuri Pasha, liberated the southwest, which became the independent republic of Azerbaidjan with Baku as its capital. This independence unfortunately did not last long, for in 1921 the Soviet Red Army seized the area and it is now part of the USSR.

Until rich oil wells were found, the main occupation of the tribes was breeding sheep and goats, planting cotton and producing silk, although the people had always woven rugs from the eighteenth century onwards. These were sold in Tiflis bazaar, to be shipped to Constantinople or New York by Armenian dealers who controlled the market, and many of the finest Caucasian rugs are to be found in North America today. I remember once Shovlet Aga, a Baku carpet dealer who looked after my grandfather's collection, telling him that an important sale of rugs was going to take place in Tiflis. Without asking how many pieces there were or how much they would cost, my grandfather instructed Shovlet Aga to buy them all if he felt they would enrich his collection. Everyone cried, 'Aga, the house is full of them ! There is no space to lay them on the floor !' But he answered, 'Children, there is always a place for such beauties in my house. If not on the floor, then on the walls.'

Caucasian rugs are unlike any other group as they are almost entirely geometric in design and are filled with stars, squares, diamonds fringed with hooks, angular peacocks, camels, dogs and human figures. The bright colours are boldly used in solid masses and there is no shading so typical of Persian weaving, except sometimes for an *abrash* across the field.

Armenian Koubas

In my opinion the well known *ejdaharli* or 'dragon' carpets were not made in Kouba in the Caucasus, as is widely believed, but were made near Erivan, the ancient capital of the Armenian kings and now the capital of Soviet Armenia.

The Armenian people lived in this area between the Black Sea and the Caspian Sea, south of the Caucasus in the mountains which give rise to nearly all the great rivers of western Asia, among them Mount Ararat on which the ark of Noah rested when the waters of the flood subsided. Many of the people spread into Turkey and Caucasia and the richest Armenian merchant colony was established in Kouba (itself a great trading centre where all the Armenian textiles were sold) during the sixteenth and seventeenth century, when the 'dragon' carpets were woven. As we have seen before, carpets are often given the name of the town at which they were marketed and the fact that a number of the 'dragon' Koubas are signed in Arabic and not in Armenian suggests that they were woven to order, the immigrant merchants no doubt encouraging the trade between the two countries. The design is based on a struggle between a dragon and a phoenix, formalised almost out of recognition. The same motif, treated in a more realistic manner, can be seen both in Chinese rugs and in Anatolian rugs of the fifteenth century,

H

such as the one painted by the Italian artist Domenico di Bartolo in about 1440. The carpets are large and narrow and are woven with a double knot, similar to the Indo-Ispahans of the sixteenth century. The colours are brilliant red, blue, green, yellow and white. They are very rarely seen outside museums.

Hile

Hile is the name of a small village which once belonged to our tribe, near the port of Baku and its surrounding oil fields. It was there my grandparents were born and as children, one of our greatest pleasures was to visit them, when the *Kent-Aga* (Alderman) of the village would give us small mats which were placed under our cushions at lunch. There are other villages nearby which wove rugs, such as Binagadi, Ermenkent and Surahani, but they may all be called Baku because they were sold in the Baku bazaar, although in fact no rugs were made in that town.

Hile rugs are beautiful and are noted not only for their good design but for their characteristic use of large quantities of turquoise blue, white and golden yellow. Those made by Turks have large cones completely filling the field, with a small stepped medallion in the centre, while the villagers of Armenian Ermenkent weave them with a cross inside a medallion. The rarest examples have stylised peacocks and are made by both races. The oldest Hiles date from the eighteenth century and are closely woven, the colours having a 'dusty' tone which gives a delicate softness.

Surahani

Weaving of these small rugs began during the middle of the eighteenth century and had ended by the first half of the nineteenth. During the last seven years I have only seen two, one sold to Ulrich Schurmann, which he illustrates in his last book on Caucasian rugs,* pl. no. 88, p. 243, and the other to Ibrahim bey Beyhum, Director of the Sursock Museum in Beirut. The Surahani weavers use simple geometric shapes in dark brown, black, light green and occasional patches of red and white.

Gendje

The city where these originated has been renamed Elizabethpol by the Russians, but the rugs continue to be called by their old name. They are long and narrow with a coarse weave in red, green, orange and black and, although they have no traditional design of their own, they are often found with diagonal bands of colour sprigged with flowers or cones.

* *Caucasian Rugs*, Allen & Unwin.

Susha

These are woven in the northern part of the Karabag district. They are renowned
for their highly artistic development of cone, bird, animal and plant forms within
ornamental filigree borders. Usually long and narrow, the best rugs were made
in the eighteenth century. The colours are magenta, white, indigo blue, a little
black and sometimes a small amount of turquoise blue and yellow.

Seichur

They are woven in the Kouba area and are sometimes mistakenly called Georgian.
They are closely knotted and have long leaves forming a trellis, or rows of poppies
and roses in the European taste. Their strong colouring includes blue, black, red
and yellow and the outer borders have a running scroll design similar to that
found in Soumaks.

Derbent

Named after the city of Derbent, these are similar in design and colouring to
Shirvans although they are much coarser. The dark field is filled with palmettes
and stylised lilies in blue, red, green and yellow and the borders, like those of
Shirvans, often have mock Kufic lettering.

Karabagh

The city of the Black Garden, Karabag (Kara Dagh) is on the northern slopes of
the mountain range which marks the frontier between Persia and Russia. Armenians settled there in the eighteenth century and most of the rugs are signed in
Armenian and dated in Western figures. There is a very strong French influence
to be seen and many of the rugs are woven with roses and strapwork in the style
of French Aubussons and Savonneries. An unusual type of Karabag is worked
with green or yellow parrots on a magenta, ink blue or black ground, but the
oldest and rarest are called a *kostum*, a set of four rugs. So rare are they that I have
never yet been able to find one during the time I have spent dealing in carpets.
A Karabag *kostum* is woven in camel hair, the brown ground filled with black
roses and green leaves within three or four narrow floral borders.

Kazak (Kazah)

Woven in the vast plain between Georgia and Karabag, their name has nothing
to do with the Russian Cossacks who have proved so troublesome to Turks.
Kazaks are large in size and bold in design and are one of the most individual and

striking of Oriental rugs. Only wool is used, and the pile is thick and heavy. Woven with the Ghiordes knot, the patterns are simple, and areas of unbroken red, white and green are massed together. The border design is often a wineglass shape alternating with a leaf, or else with crab-like creatures set claw to claw. Many Kazaks are dated, the majority are around sixty to seventy years old, but antiques are found, their pile partly dyed yellow. There is an excellent type of Kazak called *bordijali* (eagle) which has two or three large medallions filling the field resembling double-headed eagles with outstretched wings.

Shirvan

The Khans of Shirvan in the seventeenth and eighteenth centuries played an important role in the history of Caucasia, and the Shirvan district, rich in cotton, wool and silk, became the residential area for the Turkish nobility and the cross-road between Georgia, Armenia, Turkey and Persia. Fine *kelims* and prayer rugs were woven on commission with religious symbols such as the Hand of Fatima, water ewers and combs. The most highly esteemed rugs were partly in silk, with Arabic inscriptions, and another rare type was made for the Khan's palace, with a throne in the field. The principal colours of the short-piled Shirvans are deep blue, ivory, olive green and deep red, the field filled with formal flowerheads, lilies, plants, peacocks or jewellery, and the borders often have an adaptation of Kufic lettering, found in the Oushak rugs of the sixteenth century.

Kabistan

There is no true Kabistan rug. The name may have been a corruption of Koubistan, but I consider them to be the best rugs from the Shirvan area, often taken by Mohammedans on their pilgrimage to Mecca.

Talish

To the south lies the province of Talish with its city port, Lenkoran. No older than the nineteenth century, Talish rugs are long and narrow, the plain fields in rich red or green. The borders, often in yellow or cream, are most distinctive with a large flowerhead alternating with four smaller flowerheads, which form a square.

Mugan

In the West collectors do not value Mugans highly, but in the Orient they are esteemed because of their softness to the feet. Made by nomadic tribes from the steppes of Mugan, the earliest examples were woven some time in the nineteenth century. They are similar to Talish, but the fields have two or three rows of

A Seichur rug

A Karabagh rug, dated
and inscribed in
Armenian

A Karabagh rug with
parrots

A 'bordijali' Kazak rug

(*opposite*) Borders of
Caucasian rugs with 'crab'
pattern and 'wine glass'
and leaf designs

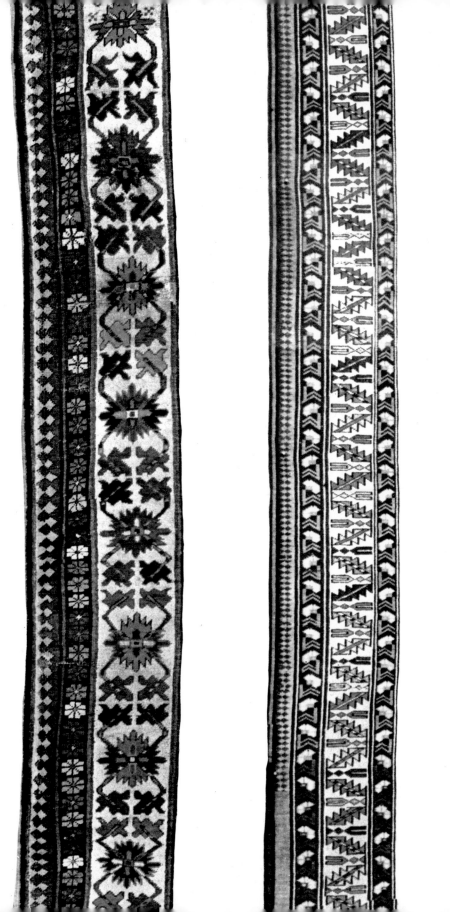

A Daghestan prayer rug

(*opposite*) A Talish rug

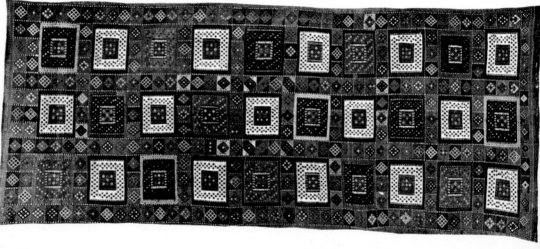

octagons or squares edged with hooks. They are either small, or long and narrow, and the vegetable dyes are bright blue, red, green and yellow.

Dagestan

The people living in the plain of Dagestan were not only courageous and spirited defenders of their land, but great craftsmen. Many different names have been given to their work, such as Sheki-Shemaha and Lezgi, but the true Dagestan is a beautiful small prayer rug with a golden yellow *mihrab* woven with a trellis of stars, cones, flowers or birds. The best vegetable dyes are used in clear bright colours and the finely knotted pile is very closely clipped.

Tchitchi (Chichi)

These small rugs, of excellent quality, are woven with a pattern of hooked stars or flowerheads so tightly packed together that they resemble a mosaic. The borders have a distinctive design of flowerheads with a ribbon running through them. The most usual colouring is a soft buff, grey and yellow against a dark blue ground.

Caucasian Kouba

Kouba has already been discussed as having been the trading centre for Armenian carpets but it produced as well much excellent work in the eighteenth and nineteenth centuries. Koubas are either long rugs or prayer rugs with a bold all-over design of flowerheads with flame-like edges in white, blue, yellow and turquoise on an indigo blue or black ground, made from the best vegetable dyes. Since the corrosive black dye eats away the wool, the flowers themselves are left standing out in relief, giving an even sharper definition to the already brilliant colours.

Soumak

Although Soumaks are superficially like the flat, pileless *kelims*, they are not double-faced and reversible, but have loose threads hanging from the back in the style of a European tapestry. Despite their lack of pile, Soumaks are extremely durable and hard-wearing, being woven from a tightly-spun woollen yarn. In the East they are used as divan covers or for the floors to houses to which people move during the summer, often taking the place of a table when meals are eaten out of doors.

Soumaks are woven with a series of flattened octagonal medallions, the remainder of the field being scattered with many nomadic devices. The outer border is always worked with forward-slanting scrolls, like waves. The ground colour is a faded madder red or blue, although the rarest are in yellow, and the patterns are in darkish blue with a little white, brown, yellow and green.

(*opposite above*) A Kouba prayer rug
(*opposite below*) A Verné rug

Kelims

Caucasian *kelims* are usually made in one piece and come from the Shirvan district. There are three grades, *palas*, *verné* and the best quality *zilli* (*silé*). I remember that as children in my grandparent's house, we used to enjoy sitting round a table which was covered by one of these beautiful *zillis*, warming ourselves by a charcoal-filled brazier as we listened to stories during the long winter evenings.

index